School RULES!

projects

planning and polishing pointers
to make you a project pro

by Emma MacLaren Henke
illustrated by Nikki Upsher

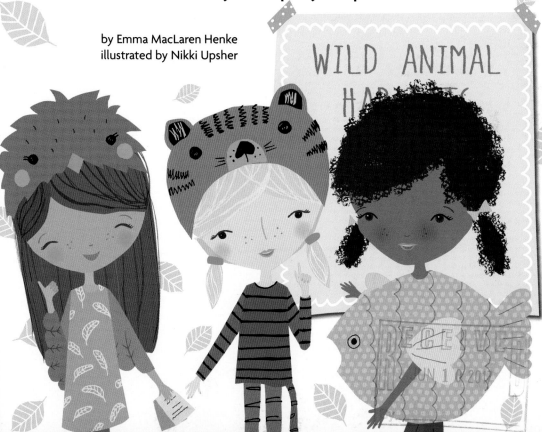

WILD ANIMAL

Published by American Girl Publishing

17 18 19 20 21 22 23 24 LEO 10 9 8 7 6 5 4 3 2 1

Editorial Development: Darcie Johnston
Art Direction & Design: Sarah Jane Boecher
Production: Jeannette Bailey, Caryl Boyer, Cynthia Stiles, Kristi Tabrizi
Illustrations: Nikki Upsher
Special thanks to Tanya Zempel, elementary education consultant

Library of Congress Cataloging-in-Publication Data
Names: Henke, Emma MacLaren, author. | Upsher, Nikki, illustrator.
Title: School rules! Projects : planning and polishing pointers to make you a project pro /
by Emma MacLaren Henke ; illustrated by Nikki Upsher.
Description: Middleton, WI : American Girl Publishing, 2017. | Series: School rules!
Identifiers: LCCN 2016025587 (print) | LCCN 2016044404 (ebook) |
ISBN 9781683370017 (pbk.) | ISBN 9781683370048 (ebook) | ISBN 9781683370048 (epub)
Subjects: LCSH: Report writing—Juvenile literature. | Research—Juvenile literature. |
Girls—Life skills guides—Juvenile literature.
Classification: LCC LB1047.3 .H46 2017 (print) | LCC LB1047.3 (ebook) | DDC 808.02—dc23
LC record available at https://lccn.loc.gov/2016025587

americangirl.com/service

Dear Reader,

School projects can feel like a very big deal. When you're faced with a research report to write, a model to make, or a presentation to prepare, it's hard to know where to start.

Whatever kind of project you're working on, the secret to success (and to keeping your cool) is making a plan. This book will guide you step-by-step, whether you're reporting on wild animal habitats, dressing like an ancient Egyptian, or staging a super science experiment. You'll discover the best ways to keep track of your ideas, your materials, and your time. You'll learn how to brainstorm and choose topics. You'll find tips for doing research and advice for getting the right kind of help.

Projects let your creative side shine. They let you learn by doing and by exploring your own interests. Best of all, you can have fun along the way! We'll show you how.

Your Friends at American Girl

contents

Yippee

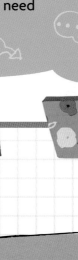

Polish your project, work with a team,
and solve project problems.

THE PROJECT PROCESS

Follow these steps to make a plan for any project assignment.

MOTIVATION METER

What's your attitude toward tackling tough projects?

1. This morning, your teacher handed out the assignment sheet for a five-page report due in three weeks. By lunchtime you've . . .
   a. made a list of possible topics and a daily plan for completing the report on time.
   b. started to think about a topic.
   c. stuffed the assignment sheet in your locker. You don't need it yet—three weeks is far away!

2. Thinking about the six book reports due by Thanksgiving makes you feel . . .
   a. excited! You've read some great books, and you've already got four done.
   b. a little nervous. You've read some great books, but you've got to figure out what to write.
   c. completely overwhelmed. You haven't even visited the library, and the due date is less than a month away.

3. Your teacher asks for your help planning a class celebration. You begin by . . .
   a. brainstorming themes and recruiting friends to make snacks.
   b. asking your friends what they think the party should be like.
   c. dreaming about the delicious party food. Mmm . . . pizza!

4. You're working on a group project for history class: a skit about the American Revolution. When it's one week till showtime, you've made sure your group has . . .
   a. written the skit, made the costumes, and memorized lines.
   b. come up with a clever skit. Now you need to assign the parts and learn the lines.
   c. had fun working on the project. You haven't gotten much done on the skit, but you and your pals are now champs at your dad's vintage pinball machine.

PROJECTS

CRAFTS

NATURE

5. You decided to dress up as Marie Curie for the science fair, but your outfit's not turning out as you planned. You decide to . . .

a. ask your parents and school librarian for help. If the librarian steers you in the right direction, your mom can help you sew a cool costume.

b. borrow a lab coat from your neighbor who's a pharmacist and ask your mom to help you find pictures of Marie Curie.

c. throw on one of your dad's white shirts, pretend it's a lab coat, and call it a day.

Answers

Give yourself 3 points for each **a** answer you chose, 2 points for each **b**, and 1 point for every **c**, and add up your score.

However you score, if you plan your time and break your project down into small tasks, you can complete any assignment with success. Tend to dawdle or delay when you're faced with a challenging project? You're not alone! Try these tactics to get up to speed and keep at it till you reach the finish line.

12-15
A+ project prepper

5-7
project procrastinator

8-11
MAKING PROJECT PROGRESS

Use a calendar to organize your tasks, and check off the days as they pass.

Ask a family member or friend to keep you on track.

Break your project down into small steps. Reward yourself—call a friend, pet your cat, have a treat—after each step you complete.

Use to-do lists. Check off each item after you do it—and enjoy the sense of satisfaction!

Set aside a specific time each day to work and review your progress.

9

Know Before You Go

The best way to begin? Read the directions, highlighting the four kinds of info you need to know.

Social Studies
Unit 3
Ms. Cronos

Greek God or Goddess Research Project

To conclude our study of Greek mythology, your assignment is to research a Greek god or goddess who interests you and create a report that includes a class presentation.

You'll write a 300- to 500-word report about your god or goddess, accompanied by a visual presentation of your research, such as a poster, slide show, model, or costume.

Be ready to present your project in class on Monday, February 23. You'll summarize your report in a one-minute speech and share your visual presentation.

Big Picture

This is what you're supposed to do and what you'll turn in when you're done.

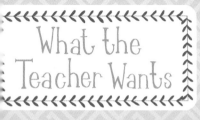

What the Teacher Wants

Look for the specific details about different parts of the assignment.

• How long should your report be?
• What items do you need to include?
• What should your project look like?

Examples

You can use your teacher's suggestions, but don't be afraid to be creative. Check with your teacher if you have questions about your idea.

Due Date

Write your project due date in your planner as soon as you get the assignment. Sometimes teachers set separate due dates for different parts of the project. Be sure to mark each one.

As you work on your project, check the assignment details every few days—not just at the beginning and the end. That way you can be sure you're doing all the right things and keeping up the pace. If there's a detail you're not sure about, ask your teacher instead of guessing. Teachers want you to succeed!

LIGHTNING STRIKES!

Spark ideas for your project with brainstorming.

When you **brainstorm,** you write down whatever ideas come to mind during a short period of time—just 5 or 10 minutes. Don't judge! Simply write every thought down. When you're done, pick out the ideas you like best.

Here are three different ways to brainstorm. Use them all to choose your general topic, and then pinpoint a specific idea for your project.

LIST IT

To choose a topic, just write all your ideas in a list. If you like, add a few words about why each idea interests you. Then look at your list and decide which idea appeals to you the most.

Zeus
he's in charge

Athena
wisdom—that's cool
helped heroes
city of Athens

Aphrodite
goddess of love

Janus two faces
Do I have to write
two reports?
Oops!
NOT GREEK
can't do anyway

Artemis
goddess of hunt
bow & arrow?
animals—
I love animals!

MAP IT

After you've chosen a topic, use it to make a mind map. Start by writing your topic in the middle of a blank sheet of paper and circling it. Then write thoughts *about* the topic around it. Use lines to connect any thoughts that are related to each other. Include ideas, facts, and even questions in your mind map—they will help guide your research later on.

QUESTION IT

Now brainstorm a list of questions that you'd like to answer about your topic, starting with the basics:

WHO?
Greek goddess or god—Athena. Also, who were her friends and enemies among the other gods?

WHAT?
Goddess of wisdom, war. What else did she represent?

WHEN?
A long time ago!!! (In what years did ancient Greeks worship her most?)

WHERE?
Ancient Greece. Was she worshipped anyplace else?

HOW?
How did she get her powers? How did she help heroes?

WHY?
Why was she so popular and adored?

Jot down answers if you know them, and use unanswered questions as a starting point for your research.

Here's another important question: WHAT DO I WANT TO KNOW MORE ABOUT?

If you're interested in your topic, you'll have fun working on your project. And if you care about your topic, your teacher and classmates will probably care, too.

When you're sure of your topic, come up with a final question that helps you pinpoint the main idea of your project. Here are some examples . . .

Why was Athena so important to the people of Athens?

How did Athena become associated with olives, owls, and her other symbols?

How did the other gods see Athena? How did she fit in among them?

THE RIGHT IDEA

Answer these questions to make sure your topic is *juuust* right.

~~Greek goddesses~~

300-500 words? I could only say a little bit about a few goddesses.

~~Athena's owl~~

How much can I really find out about this bird?

Athena's Owl

~~Athena is the goddess of wisdom.~~

Um, nothing new here.

Why was Athena so important to Athens?

THIS IS IT!

Wisdom
Courage
Strength

Is it too broad?
Is there too much info to fit in my project?

Is it too narrow?
Will I run out of things to say?

Is it too simple?
Will I just be saying what people already know?

Will it let me ask questions and discover new things, or just list facts?

Why is this such a good topic? Because it allows you to give general information about Athena but also find out something more: the reasons why the goddess was so important to the people of ancient Athens. It also lets you form ideas and opinions, and it gives readers a chance to form them, too.

15

DIVIDE anD conQuer

Break down your project into steps,
and then set a schedule for completing each one.

As soon as you receive the assignment, read through it carefully and find out exactly what you need to do. Make a list of the parts.

Next, make a list of supplies you'll need. Gather what you have, and ask your parents or teacher for help getting the rest.

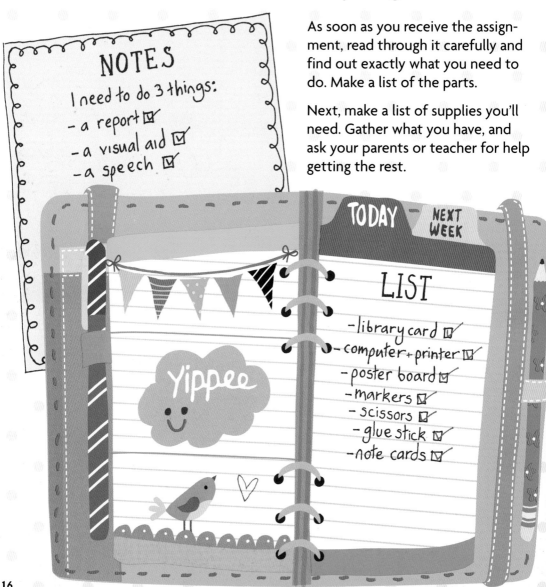

NOTES

I need to do 3 things:
- a report ☑
- a visual aid ☑
- a speech ☑

TODAY   NEXT WEEK

Yippee

LIST

- library card ☑
- computer + printer ☑
- poster board ☑
- markers ☑
- scissors ☑
- glue stick ☑
- note cards ☑

Mark the due date on your calendar or planner. Then, working backward from that date, schedule the smaller steps you'll take to complete your project.

BRAINSTORM: Generate and refine your ideas. Come up with questions that you'll research.

RESEARCH: Read books, online articles, and other sources. Take notes and organize them. Try to find answers to your research questions. Figure out how the information you find fits into your project.

CREATE: Draft your report, lay out your poster, write your speech, build your model.

REVIEW, EDIT & PRACTICE:
Give yourself time to review your work. Edit and proofread your writing, practice your performance, and put finishing touches on posters and models.

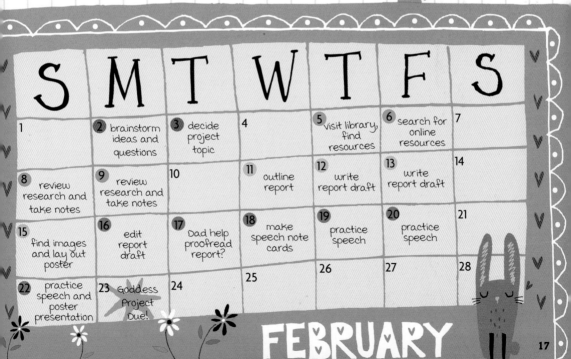

S	M	T	W	T	F	S
1	2 brainstorm ideas and questions	3 decide project topic	4	5 visit library, find resources	6 search for online resources	7
8 review research and take notes	9 review research and take notes	10	11 outline report	12 write report draft	13 write report draft	14
15 find images and lay out poster	16 edit report draft	17 Dad help proofread report?	18 make speech note cards	19 practice speech	20 practice speech	21
22 practice speech and poster presentation	23 Goddess Project Due!	24	25	26	27	28

FEBRUARY

17

WHAT'S YOUR PROJECT POWER?

Report? Speech? Model? Poster? Sometimes your teacher lets you choose! Which project style suits you best?

1. At school, one subject where you're a star student is . . .
   a. public speaking. Your speech style sets a high bar.
   b. art. Your paintings and sculptures earn great grades.
   c. English. You love writing essays, stories, and book reports.

2. Your mom needs your help getting ready for your family reunion. You'd volunteer to . . .
   a. write a letter urging far-flung relatives to make the trip.
   b. create a scrapbook that highlights all the branches of your brood.
   c. plan a skit about your family's talents, hobbies, and quirks.

3. The after-school activity that calls your name is . . .
   a. improv comedy club.
   b. writer's workshop.
   c. pottery studio.

4. You'd enjoy earning a scout badge called . . .
   a. Creative Crafter: you could sew, make jewelry, and model with clay.
   b. Drama Dreamer: you could perform a soliloquy, dress in costume, and write a skit.
   c. Story Scout: you could write a short story and start a troop book group.

5. You want to create a special surprise for your best friend's birthday. You'd decide to . . .
   a. knit a scarf in her favorite color.
   b. write her a personalized poem.
   c. prep all your pals to perform a singing telegram birthday wish.

Answers

Did you choose mostly **blue?** Your project power is writing. That's a superpower, because most projects require you to research and write at least a little.

BRANCH OUT!

Tired of reports and posters? Try these creative ways to show what you know!

* Build a board game.
* Write and perform a skit.
* Produce your own digital video.
* Showcase photos you take yourself in a collage or slide show.
* Create a crossword or word search.
* Construct a diorama.

Did you pick **purple** the most? Your project power is performing. When you can, you like to present projects as a speech, skit, or show. You can use your performer's polish to perk up reports, posters, and models, too.

Did you go with mostly **green?** Your project power is creating. You'd choose hands-on projects that let you make models, costumes, dioramas, posters, and more. Try planning your steps to "build" reports and speeches the same way you plan the projects you craft or create.

Many school projects call on all three powers. Make the most of your top strength, but don't be afraid to try something new. School projects teach you as much about planning and working on your own as they do about the subject you study.

STOCK UP!

Keep these supplies on hand for a head start on any project.

pens

pencils

markers

MARKER

sticky notes
Make notes in books and on print-outs, posters, and models.

spiral notebook or composition book
Keep ideas and notes for a project together in one place!

NOTES

highlighters
Highlight research info on printouts and photocopies.

HIGHLIGHTER

construction or scrapbooking paper

scissors

NOTES

ruler
Cut along a straight edge. Measure perfect placement for poster images.

tape

note cards
Use them for taking notes and giving presentations.

paper

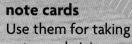

computer and printer
If you don't have them at home, use them at your school or library.

library card
Your most important project tool!

glue sticks

poster board

LIBRARY CARD

GLUE STICK

REALITY CHECK

Can you tell if your big idea is *too* big?
Ask yourself these **questions** to find out.

What do I already know, and what will I be able to learn?

Your project is a presentation on American Sign Language. But you don't know any sign language yourself. You'd plan to . . .

a. teach your classmates how to tell a joke in sign language.

b. show your class how to spell your name and say please and thank you in sign language.

How much time do I have?

You're writing fiction for English, and you have a great story idea. Your next writing project is due in three weeks. You'd decide to . . .

a. expand your idea into a multi-chapter novel.

b. use your idea to write and polish a 1,000-word short story.

What supplies do I need, and how much will they cost?

You need to build a model of an Egyptian pyramid for your world history class. You'd decide to . . .

a. ask your mom to take you to the toy store to buy that detailed gold-block pyramid building set you saw on TV. It costs $199.99, but wow! It will be so beautiful when it's done.

b. figure out what you can do with heavy-duty cardboard from the recycling bin and gold paint from the garage.

> Who else do I need to involve, and how will I organize their help?

Your teacher wants you to "perform" a book report. You'd choose to . . .

a. stage a scene from your book that takes place at a crowded party. You'll recruit all your classmates to act as extras!

b. memorize a monologue from the main character of your book and recite it in class.

> Where will I get help if I need it?

Time for the science fair. You'd plan to research . . .

a. brain chemistry. You live in a university town, and you know there's a brain science lab on campus. They'll let you in and help with your project, right?

b. which materials are the best conductors of electricity. Your mom is an electrical engineer, so she should be able to help.

Answers

Did you choose any a's? If so, you might need a reality check! Before you invest your time or money in a project, review the **questions** to make sure your idea is one you can handle. Don't get in over your head!

Reduce, Reuse, Recycle
Keep project costs down by searching for supplies around the house. Check out . . .

closets and costume bins. Dressing up as Bessie Coleman? See if you can borrow your dad's leather bomber jacket and your brother's swim goggles. Clara Barton? Maybe you could wear the lab coat from your mad scientist Halloween costume.

the family craft bin. Jazz up your poster or model with glitter glue, felt cutouts, and even feathers!

the recycling bin. Heavy cardboard boxes make sturdy backing material for posters. Cut, glue, and paint cardboard shapes to make architectural models.

the toy box. Use interlocking blocks to create custom models. Use toy animals, action figures, or doll furniture in dioramas.

gift wrap. Use wrapping paper as a poster background. Tissue paper, ribbons, and bows can enhance costumes, too.

PROJECTS THAT SHINE

Get tips to ace any kind of project, from reports and posters to models and speeches.

Reasoned Research Reports

Support your ideas with evidence to tell a convincing story.

Writing a research report is a lot like telling a story. You need a beginning, a middle, and an end. And you need to make sure readers can follow your thoughts at each point along the way.

BEGINNING

MIDDLE

END

Start with an **introduction** that tells your readers the main idea of your report and why that idea is interesting or important. In other words, tell them what you're going to tell them! To grab their attention from the first sentence, try beginning with a quote, question, or interesting fact.

opening question

main idea

Athena and Athens

Did you know that the Parthenon, the most famous monument of ancient Greece, is a temple to the goddess Athena? The ancient Athenians worshipped and admired Athena for many reasons. As the goddess of wisdom, she stood for something that Athenians were proud of. As the goddess of war, she fought for justice, which the Athenians believed in. And according to Greek mythology, Athena gave the olive tree to the city of Athens so that she could become the city's goddess.

Athena competed with Poseidon, the Greek god of the seas, to become the god who represented Athens. Both gods gave the city a gift. Poseidon created a fountain of salt water. It was

MIDDLE

Fill the middle—or **body**—of your report with **evidence** that supports your main idea. Your assignment may tell you how many examples, reasons, or facts to provide. If your teacher doesn't give you specific guidelines, though, try to include at least three pieces of evidence.

evidence (reasons, examples, or facts)

Athena competed with Poseidon, the Greek god of the seas, to become the god who represented Athens. Both gods gave the city a gift. Poseidon created a fountain of salt water. It was pretty, but the people could not drink from it or use the water to grow plants. Athena gave the city the olive tree. Her gift provided food, wood, oil, and other things.

Athens was the center of learning for ancient Greece. It makes sense that people of the city would admire the goddess of wisdom. Mythology says that Athena used her wisdom to create or inspire some of the most useful skills and tools in ancient Greece, such as weaving and pottery. Athenians relied on Athena's gifts every day.

As the goddess of war, Athena inspired the Athenians to use their minds to win battles and other contests. Athena stood for fighting wars for just reasons, not for the sake of battle. Athenians believed in fighting wars for justice.

END

At the end—or **conclusion**—of your report, restate your main idea. Then review or summarize the evidence and answer any remaining questions. For an ending that is interesting and strong, make a final point or remind your readers of the beginning of the report.

restatement of main idea

review of evidence

Athena was loved by the people of Athens for many reasons. She gave the city the olive tree, an important resource. She was wise, and ancient Athenians valued wisdom. She fought for justice and with reason, as the people of Athens hoped to do. The Athenians admired their city's goddess so much that they built a huge temple and monument to her: the Parthenon. It still stands today, reminding everyone who sees it of their love for Athena.

reminder of opening question

THE END!

29

opinion or evidence?

When you write a research report, you use **evidence**— or facts—to support your opinions. In each pair below, can you tell which statement is evidence and which is opinion?

In Greek mythology, Athena was the goddess of wisdom, war, and solving conflicts with reason.

Athena is the most interesting Greek god because she represented war and peace at the same time.

Rabbits make the best pets for people who live in apartments because they are quiet and they can be trained to use a litter box.

Rabbits are quiet pets that can be trained to use a litter box.

1.

2.

The government of the United States is made up of three branches: the legislative, the judicial, and the executive.

The judicial branch of our federal government is less important in making laws than the legislative branch or the executive branch.

Grand Canyon National Park is the most beautiful place in America.

Grand Canyon National Park is known the world over for its beauty.

3.

4.

Meriwether Lewis's discoveries in the Louisiana Territory are the most significant ever made by an American explorer.

Meriwether Lewis explored the land acquired by the United States in the Louisiana Purchase and kept detailed records of what he discovered there.

5.

answers

The statements in **green** are **facts.** That makes them evidence. The **blue** statements are **opinions.** Each opinion statement is a judgment, belief, or feeling that is based on facts but is not a fact itself. Words like *best, worst, important,* and *beautiful* signal that a statement is opinion. Your opinions are what make a report your own, and your audience wants to know what you think, so do include them! Just be sure to support them with evidence in any research project.

POSTERS THAT POP

Communicate your message at a glance with a great poster.

Posters can instantly capture your audience's attention and draw them into your topic. The purpose of a poster is to give an overview of your ideas. You don't need to include every fascinating fact you've discovered—save those details for your report or speech.

Get ready to glue with these steps:

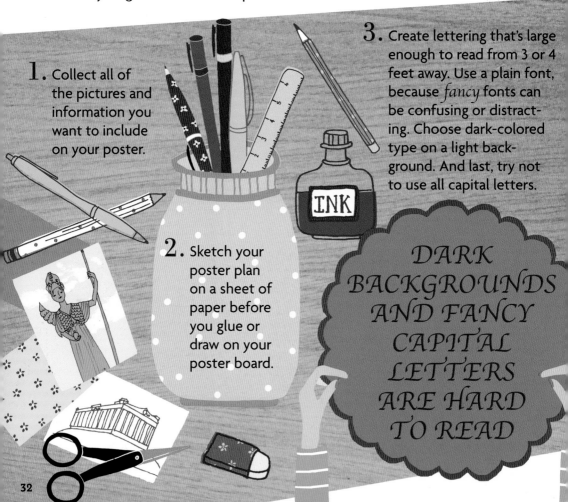

1. Collect all of the pictures and information you want to include on your poster.

2. Sketch your poster plan on a sheet of paper before you glue or draw on your poster board.

3. Create lettering that's large enough to read from 3 or 4 feet away. Use a plain font, because *fancy* fonts can be confusing or distracting. Choose dark-colored type on a light background. And last, try not to use all capital letters.

INK

DARK BACKGROUNDS AND FANCY CAPITAL LETTERS ARE HARD TO READ

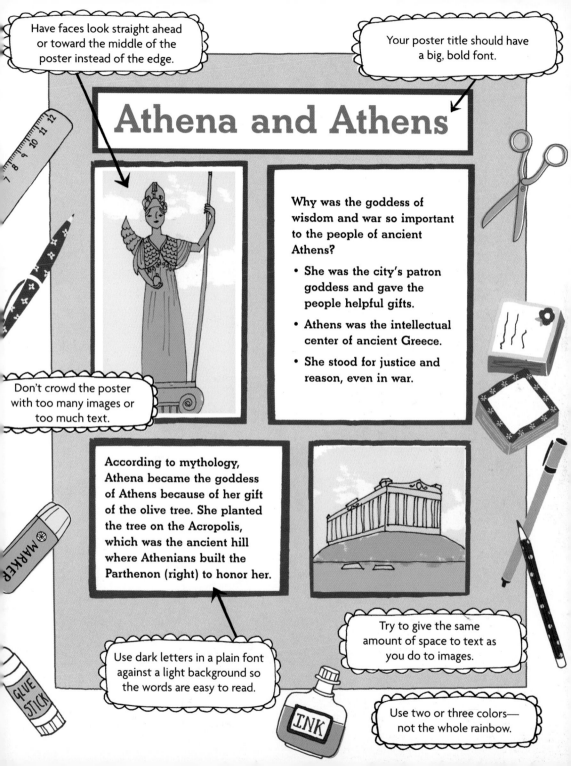

TOOLS OF THE TRADE

Add polish to your poster with the right equipment.

POSTER BOARD BASICS

Use a sturdy poster board that can stand on its own. A poster that flops over halfway through your presentation distracts from your ideas. If you need a large area for your information, use a trifold poster board. Add support to a flimsy poster board by gluing thick cardboard to the back.

WAYS WITH WORDS

Use a computer and printer to create text for your poster. Your text will be consistent, neat, and easy to read. Not sure how large to make your letters? Follow the guidelines on the next page.

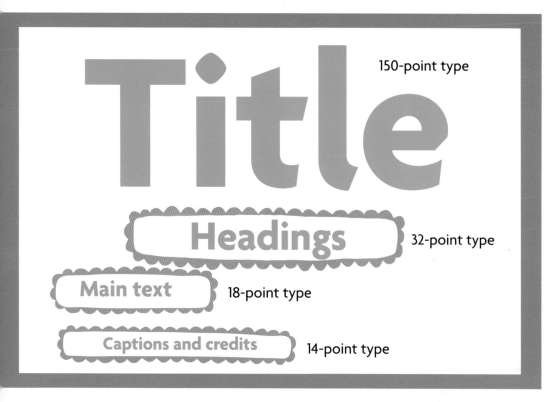

Title — 150-point type

Headings — 32-point type

Main text — 18-point type

Captions and credits — 14-point type

OUTSTANDING COLORS

Place your printed text on colored construction paper backgrounds. This helps your text stand out, especially if you're using a white poster board.

EXACTING EDGES

Ask your parents for help cutting out photos, pictures, and text with a straight edge and utility knife. Or use a straight edge and pencil to draw cutting guidelines around images and text, and use scissors to cut along the guidelines. Straight, even cuts make your poster look sharp!

FLAT ATTACHMENTS

Firmly attach text and images to your poster board with a glue stick or double-sided tape. Avoid liquid glue, because it can make your paper warp and wrinkle.

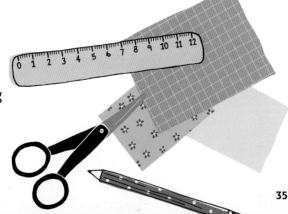

POSTER PERFECT?

Not every project idea makes a powerful poster.
Choose the project in each pair that could be
turned into the more successful poster.

1. a. information about family
      life in ancient Greece

   b. a family tree of ancient
      Greek gods and goddesses

2. a. how to fold a basic paper
      airplane

   b. how to fold an origami
      crane

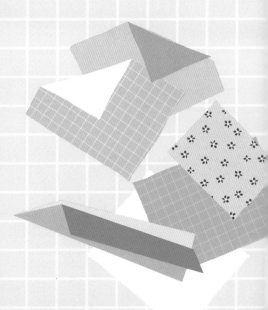

3. a. the history of your family name

b. the countries where your ancestors lived

4. a. an interpretation of a Shakespeare sonnet

b. a diagram of Shakespeare's Globe Theatre

5. a. the meaning of the parts of the American flag

b. the meaning of the words in the national anthem

answers

The best topics for posters have a strong but simple visual element. That means you can clearly "see" a few pictures in your imagination. Some ideas, like the meaning of a poem or song, are easier to explore with words than images, so a paper or speech is a better choice. And some ideas, even if they are visual, are too complicated or require too many steps to show in a poster. For those ideas, plan a demonstration instead.

super speeches

Follow a few script-writing secrets for a polished performance of any oral report.

Every great speech begins with great writing. Plan and research an oral report just like you would a written version, and then craft a draft that includes . . .

beginning
Tell your main idea.

Middle
Explain the supporting evidence.

end
Summarize or restate what you've said.

Begin your speech with an attention-getter. You might . . .

tell a story

According to mythology, Athena became the goddess of Athens in a contest . . .

use humor

Athena wasn't born in the regular way. She burst from Zeus's head! Ouch!

ask a question

Picture the Parthenon! Did you know it's a temple to the goddess Athena?

You could also start with a surprising fact, or share a quote, or come up with your own attention-grabbing idea.

SHOW AND TELL

With an oral report, you can *show* while you tell. If you have props, a costume, a demonstration, or other visual aids that make your report more interesting or your ideas easier to share, ask your teacher if you can use them. They can help you communicate. Plus, having something to do or to hold can help calm any jitters you might be feeling!

TALKING TIP

Use conversational language when you write a speech. Write it the way you would naturally say it.

Projects

WRAPPING UP

Just like you do in a written report, end your speech with a summary of your ideas. Then leave your audience with a question or quote to ponder— or with a good laugh!

Practice Makes a Performance

You've finished writing your report. Now what?

You could call it done and just stand in front of the class, reading straight from your paper. But that's not a true oral report. It's probably not what your teacher is expecting, and it's kind of boring for the audience. How can you make it a speech—or even a performance?

Card Tricks

With note cards—*presto!*—a written report is transformed into a speech. Read through your draft, picking out the big ideas and transferring them to cards, one idea per card.

Don't include every word from your report—write only enough to help you remember each point you want to make. Why? Jotting notes or bullet points instead of copying word-for-word helps you *speak* your speech instead of just reading it. It frees you to talk to your audience and connect with your eyes, your face, your voice, and your gestures.

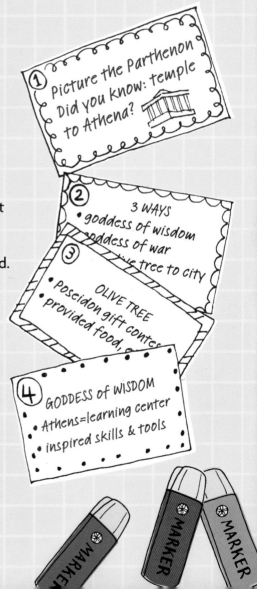

① Picture the Parthenon
Did you know: temple to Athena?

② 3 WAYS
• goddess of wisdom
• goddess of war
• ...us tree to city

③ OLIVE TREE
• Poseidon gift conte...
• provided food,...

④ GODDESS of WISDOM
• Athens=learning center
• inspired skills & tools

TIP
Number your cards so you can find your place if you get lost!